Soul Existence

Soul Existence

HILLARY R. CARRAWAY

authorHOUSE®

AuthorHouse™
1663 Liberty Drive
Bloomington, IN 47403
www.authorhouse.com
Phone: 1 (800) 839-8640

Published by AuthorHouse 09/26/2015

ISBN: 978-1-5049-5043-5 (sc)
ISBN: 978-1-5049-5041-1 (hc)
ISBN: 978-1-5049-5042-8 (e)

Library of Congress Control Number: 2015915298

Print information available on the last page.

Table of Contents

This book is dedicated to all the people I love, all those who have helped to broaden my understanding of this life and helped in forming the person that I am. Especially to my 3 amazing children and to my Husband who consistently remind me that this life, though challenging is a great gift.

Foreword

I remember lying in bed as a child and asking myself if I truly existed in that moment. Was I really there—alive? Was this who I was? Panic would set in, and after disputing the fact that I indeed existed in that moment and was confined to the boundaries of this life and body, the panic would fade and I would eventually arrive to acceptance. As I grew older, these episodes persisted, but I was usually able to push the emotions to the back of my mind because I knew the outcome, thus sparing myself the anxiety.

Occasions like those continued to create questions in my mind that were impossible to answer. Whenever I thought I'd found a sufficient answer to calm my apprehension, it always seemed to bring up another question. The cycle was bound to repeat itself.

I don't know if everyone experiences this type of thing, but I know that we all have occurrences that are unexplainable. They usually consist of an understanding between us and the unknown and as such are difficult to explain to anyone in the same detail that we experience them. When I've tried to describe the experiences, some listeners look at me as though I've lost my mind. Others seem to recognize similar situations to what they have undergone and accept my words.

This book was written because of these unexplainable moments as well as many others that have presented themselves to me over the years. I love to think as I take walks, and one fall afternoon,

an inspiration came to me. I tried to push it aside, but it wouldn't let up. Lying in bed later that night, still unable to turn my mind off, I got up to sit at my computer and create *Soul Existence*.

I'm not a college graduate, spiritual mentor, or businesswoman. I'm a housewife and a mom—an ordinary person. But I've come to realize that none of us knows what awaits us. No religion or person can tell us exactly what heaven is or what life is. Throughout our lives, we must communicate with our creator to build an understanding of our existence more genuine than what any preacher or Bible can convey to us.

My children often ask me about heaven and about the way things are. I used to refer them to the Bible, but they never seemed fully satisfied with the answers it provided. Now when they ask me these types of questions, I tell them to search their souls to look for the answers within themselves.

I hope that this work of fiction will inspire you to keep pursuing your questions and to form a unique relationship with your creator. Religion is a wonderful thing; it gives us guidance and reassurance. But sometimes we need more than that.

I think we all question our existence at times. We may not have the capability to discover the answers, but we can find peace in knowing that there is a purpose to our lives, a definite reason we're here.

Life is consumed with questions that cannot be explained. Even the Bible, as esteemed and cherished as it is, isn't capable of answering all of them. Some would argue that its pages hold the answers to all of life's mysteries. I disagree. However, I value its contents and hold it in the highest regard.

Although religion is often created by a desire to serve God and abide by his law, it segregates us, forcing us to choose a congregation. Within this commitment, there is an obligation to abide by and

fully believe all that it stands for, thus condemning what anyone but our religious peers believe.

Many beliefs and religions scattered across the world have created wonderful, kind, God-loving people. I cannot accept that there is only one chosen religion, a select few among the masses that will be allowed to grace the majesty of heaven.

Chapter 1

In cold and darkness, my soul seemed to find light and a peace that I had never known. I wanted to die. More than ever before, I welcomed it. I knew that my time on earth was about to come to an end. Finally concluding my suffering from the plague that greed and power brought to humankind. I longed for the answers that I knew only our creator held within his existence. Only he knew why we were sent to this cruel world. For all the months I spent in captivity, one question lingered in my thoughts above all others: "Why does someone

who is handed power or a better title, no matter how slight, always turn dominating and greedy? Arrogance consumes someone like this, as if a higher power has finally deemed that he or she was meant to guide the rest. These people seem to believe their lives, their ways, and their prophecies were more significant than those of whom they were meant to serve and guide. What weakness in the rest of us allows this to happen time and time again at every different level, in every aspect of life, and within every society? It is conveyed amid families, social communities, politics, religions, and in those we choose to be our highest leaders.

Power has changed hands countless times throughout the history of the world. Has there ever been a single instance in which the outcome was not the same? Our salvation is always our destruction.

These questions boiled inside me. Moments like this always made me feel weak and insignificant,

as though I was not worthy of an answer. But now the aforementioned calmness filled my soul. It was as though all the questions I had ever had no longer concerned me. After months of cold and darkness, imprisonment, humiliation, and brutality, I would never have to face those burdens again. The darkness of my cell was replaced by light and warmth. My soul rose into a magnificent existence. Every sense was overtaken by radiance. No words can explain the freedom, weightlessness, warmth, and pure pleasure that I felt as I passed from one world into the next. Love encased me. It was like waking up from a dream and finally understanding what it means to truly exist. I was a part of something so big, special, intricate, and detailed. There were brilliant colors that I could never have imagined.

Before me, all around me, and in me, I experienced my savior, my loved ones, and my dear animals that had passed away before me. Along with all of those I wished so badly that I could have saved.

He, who in my tongue was referred to as God, was not merely a being that stood before me. He was part of me—part of all of us. This being was not just one soul but the good of all souls combined. My suffering, burdens, and despair had also belonged to him. He didn't just understand my life, he had lived it alongside me.

The Lord welcomed me and thanked me for my service on Earth. My suffering was over—my journey complete! What a glorious homecoming it was! On earth, my days were often filled with fear and sadness, but all of the pain and trials were now only a distant memory. True freedom was at hand, it could never be taken away from me.

The Lord was indeed perfection—the creator of all love, compassion, and hope. Within his existence were the answers I'd so longed for, just like I always knew they would be. He recognized the eagerness for knowledge that filled my soul, and the answers flashed before me.

I now understood that power, recognition, and success were humankind's greatest temptations and therefore our greatest downfall. During our lives on earth, they seemed to define our reasons for existing. We all wanted to better ourselves, to achieve great things, to be respected among our peers. I was now able to comprehend their deception. We crave power out of a need for recognition and perhaps even self-worth. However, the well-being of others is often grossly overlooked in this pursuit. It was a battle between free will and God's will; few ever find balance between the two.

I saw that life was much more complex than I had ever realized. There was a reason for everything, a resolution to every request. Our many differences, interpretations, and self-righteousness became inane and condescending. I understood why all religions were right in their own reasoning. They each led people to their creator and guided them in the direction they chose. Many times religion created prejudices however, more often it produces

spirituality and helps reaffirm people's connection with God and the difference between right and wrong. The images flashed so swiftly, and they thoroughly communicated love and other feelings attached to them. I realized that some people need religion to remind them that their creator was near and to bring them closer to him.

Others were more in tune with their spirituality. They worshiped the earth, the creatures, and the weather. They were thankful for their bounty, and they saw the earth as a living being. Instead of looking to the Bible or prophecy, they relied upon intuition to help them choose their paths. They looked to their creator and their ancestors to guide them.

Some didn't acknowledge religion or spirituality in any form. They had seen the torment of indifference found there and chose not to be a part of it. Science and logic guided them, not the Lord or any higher power. Always naively unaware that

science was also an avenue to their creator. He had created it especially for these people because they could only believe by seeing. In other words, their connection to God could not be an unexplained feeling or words in a holy book. These souls could only understand what they could prove or touch. They were not irrational, they only had a different method of understanding and accepting their creator. Many times, God came to them through science without their recognition of him.

There were so many beliefs, religions, and political influences represented in the images. I saw how often humans had manipulated religion to protect their heritage and beliefs or to gain power. I felt the sadness of the Lord as he reminded me of the relentless destruction and persecution that religion had caused throughout history, as in my own experience on earth. I understood that the religions themselves weren't to blame for this; rather, it was people's lack of acceptance of unfamiliar religions and ideas. Most plagued by their arrogance and

inability to compromise. They were controlled by a blinding fear that power would shift; it filled them with greed and panic. The basis that these religions were founded upon was set aside and replaced by war and despair out of a never-ending need to acquire the upper hand.

There would never be a winner of these wars or a chosen religion that would rise above the rest. There was not a particular breed of people whose souls would be saved because of what they believed in or were born into, leaving the rest damned to hell. After all, many religions are scattered across the world, and none are truer than any other. None is exempt of flaws or misguided information. I saw that the only thing that really matters is love for one another, integrity, peace, kindness, generosity— and acceptance of the unacceptable!

If all God's creations and all the ideas and beliefs in the world are not accepted, the only outcome is chaos and destruction. Over many thousands

of years, this flaw of humankind could not be mended. I now saw the reason that God and all of those who would inhabit the world helped create it in order to learn from it. Life was cruel, and at times it seemed insurmountable. But the knowledge and appreciation that our souls gained from life on earth was unmatched. No one was perfect, many didn't live out of the purest integrity or responsibility, but often the knowledge those people gained was more substantial than that of others.

I saw that great strides were made on earth over the centuries, but in all that time, we had not learned to work together with humility. Earth was not created for us to suffer, but rather for us to learn and advance in the understanding of life, compromise, and love. We were meant to learn to accept and take care of each other and to appreciate and love

the world—the earth, people, and animals. We were intended to create a balance among all living things and set all religious, racial, and political issues aside.

Chapter 2

As I sat there absorbing all of this knowledge, I was suddenly interrupted. Darkness overtook the light. It choked the air as a feeling of despair and fear replaced the calmness, and a familiar emotion arose inside of me. A void grew, separating me from the peace and light. A demonic voice reached out and screeched. Angrily, it snarled and clawed at me. As before, knowledge filled me, but this time it was dark, obscene, and tormenting. My soul felt heavy and bound. The evil of humankind flashed before me. Sensations of death, destruction,

greed, jealousy, addiction, vanity, and cruelness were swept into one mighty storm. Satan in all his hellish form surrounded me. His eyes burned with evil as they peered into my soul.

Never before had I felt so exposed and vulnerable. He knew all my weaknesses, wants, and deep desires. He reminded me of sins in my past life, and I felt his pleasure as he indulged in them. The devil no longer looked frightening but handsome and confident. His whispers filled my mind, and he wanted my soul—wanted me to let go of all my inhibitions. I felt pleasure. I could taste it. He wanted me, and he wanted to please me. He showed me how powerful I could be under his guidance. His eyes were warm and welcoming, as he revealed to me his dwelling and all those that would serve me and worship me.

For an instant, I desired all that he promised, but in the next, I felt the warmth of the Lord and saw his light pierce the dark fog that was Satan. I fell to

my knees and begged the Lord for his forgiveness. I apologized for being weak, and I wept as I told him that no matter what I faced, I would always choose him.

He lifted me and told me not to weep. He explained that I had chosen him over Satan long ago, and I was safe in his kingdom. He told me that I was his child, and he would always protect me. In flashes, I saw that Satan couldn't harm those of us who were home with our savior. Our paths had finally reached their destination. Satan could only have influence over us while we were on earth. The Lord had let me experience Satan's power in that moment only to remind me of the task that I had overcome.

All humans were exposed to Satan and given the free will to live their lives as they chose. We all made mistakes, and at times we would all suffer because of the mistakes of others. The world was not perfect; it wasn't meant to be. It was cruel and

unforgiving, but God was a part of all of us. We could always turn to him. We could choose to forgive the people whose sins infringed upon us, or we could allow their sins to fuel our own. We all knew the difference between good and evil, but Satan had countless strategies for making us lose our way. He was always present to lure us away from the Lord. The Devil showed us an easy way out, a way to deal with the pain, and a way to justify the reasoning behind our sins.

I now sensed the presence of my loved ones waiting to greet me, and though I longed to feel their embraces, I hesitated. There were so many more things I wanted to know. The Lord smiled at me, and I knew that any time I needed him, all I had to do was think of him, and he would be there.

His image vanished, and before me stood everyone who had ever touched my life and loved me, even those I never met. Excitement filled me as I realized they were not strangers. We had all been

here together before, long before our lives on earth. I had known them for all time.

Each of my loved ones looked like him- or herself. However, they were flawless and ageless, and their souls were brilliant. I realized that I could communicate with all of them at once in my mind. It was as though our souls were connected, and all that I had ever wanted to know about them was apparent. What a magnificent reunion it was! The love I felt was phenomenal; it radiated throughout my entire being. I embraced each one, and tears of joy fell down our cheeks. We reminisced of our previous time together and celebrated our long-awaited reunion. I wanted to ask some for forgiveness, but there was no need.

My childhood horse, Silver, stood before me looking more magnificent than ever before. And my old dog, Angus, was no longer gray and crippled but young and full of life. All of my beloved pets were there, and just as I had always suspected, they had

souls not much different than humans', but now we could fully comprehend one another. My most obedient friends stood by my side, no longer as pets but as wise souls who would now guide me in heaven just as they had in life.

My grandma, my idol and spiritual mentor, reached out and embraced me. I had forgotten how safe I felt in her arms, but those feelings all rushed back to me. I knew that she had always been watching over me, but it was the greatest gift to see and feel her again. In this moment, I realized that the losses I suffered on earth had created the most awe-inspiring miracle of appreciation for this, greatest of reunions.

Heaven had no boundaries or limitations. It seemed to go on forever. As I walked through this glorious place, arm-in-arm with my grandma, I found myself on a familiar dirt road. I looked up, and there was the old farmhouse she shared with my grandpa in the river bottoms. The cattle were grazing in the

meadow, and the horses raced through the trees. The high mountains were covered in snow, and a warm breeze brushed against my face. Wildlife surrounded us. I was home! As we walked through the gate and up to the doorstep, I saw Grandma's beautiful garden filled with daisies, sweet peas, sunflowers, and every kind of flower you could imagine. Each one looked divine and flawless. As I opened the door, the smell of Grandma's fresh-baked bread filled the air. Everything was just how I remembered it. Oh, how I had missed the comfort of their home.

I soon began a journey to create my own place of heaven. All I had to do was think about what I wanted and how I wanted it, and it would appear. I built a small, cozy cottage in a wide valley surrounded by mountains. A calm creek ran in front of my home, and just down the pathway sat

a small pond. Wildlife filled the landscape, and all of my animals were at home here. The weather and seasons changed from time to time, but it was never too hot or too cold.

Chapter 3

To be a soul is an amazing thing. You can transport to whatever location you wish in an instant. And you're able to communicate with others with such depth, complexity, and clarity. There are no expression of sexual feelings and no marriages. When you are connected to a soul that you have a bond with, you are so in tune with one another that it is almost as though you are one. You enjoy each other for all that you are. Jealousy doesn't exist, only love and respect for all.

Each of my loved ones was so precious and unique, and each one filled a void in my soul. Like a puzzle, each piece came together to form one…all of our knowledge and experience combined. As this was revealed to me, I saw that many pieces of the puzzle were still missing. That was when I remembered those I had left behind.

Until that moment, I was so caught up in the magnificence of heaven that I had forgotten I was released from my duties of earth, but so many people I loved were still there: my parents, my friends, and many others.

Suddenly, I was swept back to earth as an observer, and the cold world that I remembered surrounded me. In heaven, time had no meaning and therefore passed much faster than on earth. My death was very recent, and I wondered if my parents were even aware of my passing. I wanted to see what had become of my body. As I floated above it, my body now seemed so heavy and awkward as though it

was a prison for my soul during the time I was on earth.

My carcass had been tossed into a pit among dozens of other dead bodies. As I looked over my fragile, bruised remains, they were almost unrecognizable to me. Sadness filled my soul, and I wondered if I had made a difference in the world.

Chapter 4

Visions of my life flashed before me, and I was reminded of happier times, playing with my cousins at our grandparent's ranch. We were so innocent and unaware that our world was changing and with it, our people. Something evil was about to reveal itself, almost as though Satan himself stepped foot on this land, claimed it, and unleashed the wrath of hell.

I was a German woman of almost seventeen years. I was considered to be of pure blood—unlike so many of my young Jewish faith companions when

Hitler and his regime began the war. None of us could have fathomed the plague of hatred that would consume our homeland.

My father was a well-respected doctor among the Germans, my mother was a homemaker and was loved by everyone that knew her. We were considered elite, which spared us the torment that so many of our neighbors and friends faced.

Hitler had a deep disdain toward Christianity, even though his mother was a devout Catholic. Deceived and unaware of his true intentions, the Catholic Church supported him on the condition that he would sign a treaty with them. However, as his power gained momentum, so did his intent to eradicate not only Catholicism but all forms of Christianity, focusing first on eliminating all followers of Judaism.

As I grew older, my deep resentment toward politics also grew. Even though people who shared my beliefs were forced to keep those thoughts to

themselves, we were Christians, and nothing would ever change that. Most of us agreed, but many were blind to Hitler's true intentions and what he had in store for us.

My father's small medical practice was now overrun with soldiers, most of his staff was sent off to help in other regions. So very hesitantly the duty of assisting him often fell upon myself. At first I'm sure that my father found me a very inadequate assistant. I often became queasy at the site of blood and very emotionally attached to many of the situations and patients that we tended. Over time I became more resilient and learned the ways of medicine and often assisted him with surgeries and diagnoses.

My mother became the office manager and bookkeeper. We were always under close watch, but over the years we managed to help smuggle many Jews to safer locations. We lived two very separate lives, and we were always aware that if or when we

got caught, we would suffer dire consequences. But doing nothing was unthinkable!

War is gruesome, no matter why it begins. Unfortunately, until you are standing in the aftermath, it's almost impossible to foresee the waste and destruction that it leaves behind.

In my short life, I saw the most horrific and cruel acts of humankind. Ordinary people—some whom I had known my entire life—turned into monsters all because of one man's influence. Millions hailed him and millions fell to him. The value of human life was lost in the grasp of hatred, and the downfall of our world had arrived.

Chapter 5

One unusually warm autumn day, I was presented with an opportunity. Even though I was aware of its danger, there was no way I could ignore it. My father begged me not to pursue it. It was too risky, he said. He was a quiet man, studious and serious, but that day I felt the emotion behind his words. The calm energy he normally conveyed was overshadowed by a deep sense of fear.

He told me that there was only so much we could do, and if our activity was exposed, we would no longer be able to help anyone including ourselves.

His words, though appropriate, meant little to me. I was restless and tired of hiding. The war had been going on for several years with no end in sight, and everything that my family had done seemed so insignificant in comparison to the erosion that surrounded us. Those would be the last words my father would ever share with me, but in the following months I was often reminded of them.

The previous day an old German woman named Helga, who had helped us to relocate refugees in the past, came into our office. She told me that she knew of three young children who had escaped from the German soldiers days earlier, after their parents were captured. They were staying in an abandoned barn on the outskirts of town. Several people had been sneaking them food, but it was only a matter of time before they were discovered, and the harsh winter was approaching. Helga knew that I often took supplies and medicine to some of the nearby towns, and she said a family had agreed to take the children in if we could get them there.

Patrols had multiplied in recent months, and there were checkpoints on every road. But we figured that because the soldiers were used to seeing me haul supplies every week, their suspicion of me would be low. In that regard, we were right. However, when you are desperate for everything to go perfectly, it's amazing how quickly it can go wrong.

We hid the children in a large crate in the back of my truck. As I tucked them underneath the blankets and supplies, I paused to look at them for a moment longer. They were so young and calm: two boys, age twelve and ten, and a little girl, almost six. My hands shook as I adjusted everything to make it as comfortable as possible. The calmness of the two boys was uncanny. War had replaced their innocence with desperation to survive. They insisted on having their little sister lie between them. Even her demeanor, though nervous, was not what I would have expected of a young child under such harsh circumstances.

As I went to cover their faces, I wondered if I would ever see them again and if their future would be pleasant. I wanted to say something comforting, but no words came to mind that seemed fitting, I choked back my tears.

A man named Lenz that I had known casually for many years was supposed to travel several miles ahead of me. He would wait behind the building where I dropped off supplies and help me unload the cart containing the children. Then he would load the cart on to his truck to transport them to their new home.

As I drove along the dirt road, it suddenly dawned on me how precious my cargo was. The radio was full of static, and this only irritated my already stressed nerves, so I turned it off and drove in silence. I prayed to God, begging him to hear my prayer. I told him that I needed his help that day more than ever. These children needed a chance at a better life. As I prayed for them, I realized that I

hadn't even asked their names. How foolish I felt. I couldn't even say a proper prayer. I was so ill-prepared and inadequate. Why had I been chosen to transport these children? There were times when I still felt like a child myself.

Just I was about to pull over and turn my truck around because of the paralyzing fear, I looked ahead and saw a group of soldiers and vehicles. I had already reached the checkpoint—it was too late for reservations. I pulled up to the checkpoint, and much to my surprise, an acquaintance of my father's, General Otto Christophe Von Fleming, welcomed me. It was unusual for a man of his stature to be out in the field. I had met him several times at different functions over the years. I had always thought of him as a handsome man, and he had a kind presence, but I knew better than to take that nature for granted. He was a well-respected soldier and a legend of sorts in our community. There was a reason he had acquired his current

position of authority; his devotion to the Nazis was evident.

He recognized me in return and gave me a nod with a hint of a smile. In that moment, my emotions settled, and I pulled myself together. He asked me how my father was doing, and I told him that he'd been busy as always but was doing very well.

Several young soldiers were off to the side, aiming their rifles toward a meadow. They seemed to be goofing off, and I thought how unfair it was that they were forced to be there. They should have been off somewhere being boys, not soldiers. The general seemed very displeased by their lack of professionalism, and I could tell he was eager to reprimand them. We chatted for a moment longer about the unusually nice weather we had been experiencing. He asked me what I was hauling, and I told him it was the usual supplies for the surrounding towns. Just as he raised his hand to motion me forward, several loud gunshots rang

out, followed by the scarcely audible scream of a small child.

The young soldiers had spotted a rabbit in the meadow and took several shots at it. For a second, I hoped that no one else heard the scream I had, but the look in the head officer's eyes told me otherwise. Without even thinking, I stepped on the gas and sped off as fast as I could. My large truck was slow, but I would have a small lead. I prayed it would be enough to get the children to Lenz.

My hope was short-lived. In my review mirror, I saw that a small military vehicle was rapidly approaching. Rifles were pointed toward my truck, and I held my breath as I waited for bullets to shower it. Much to my surprise, the soldiers refrained from doing so. Perhaps they figured I wouldn't put up much of a fight because of my gender and age. But by this point, I was determined to get these kids to safety no matter what it took.

I had gone too far across a line. My fate was set in stone, and there was no way to amend the way they now saw me. I was a traitor. As the word echoed through my mind, its harshness was softened in my conscience. I thoroughly believed in my cause, and every fiber of my being supported what I was doing.

The military vehicle approached on my left side, and my eyes met once again with the general's. He yelled for me to pull over, but instead I swerved toward his vehicle, smashing into its side and thrusting it off the road. Dust filled my rear view mirror now, but I knew there would be more soldiers on their way. I reached for my father's pistol hidden under the seat and drove as fast as my old truck would go.

God was definitely on our side that day. Not much farther up the road, I spotted Lenz pulled over. He had noticed the unusually large plume of dust behind him and waited for me.

He could tell that we were in trouble. Without needing to exchange words, we both jumped out of our vehicles and raced to the back of my truck. The children, very shaken by this point, had pushed the lid off of the crate. With little time to spare, we helped them out. Lenz got them into his truck as I caped a large blanket over them.

Lenz grabbed my arm to assist me into his truck, but I pulled away. The soldiers already knew who I was, and someone would have to answer for what we had done. The children's only chance was Lenz, and we both knew it. His brilliant blue eyes looked compassionately at mine. His looks had always seemed plain to me, but in this life-or-death moment, I realized there was far more to this simple man than I had ever given him credit for. Regret for not getting to know him better flashed through my mind as I yelled for him to hurry. He reluctantly turned and climbed into his truck.

He and the children headed away, I got back in my truck and parked it sideways across the road to form my own roadblock. I grabbed my pistol, sat down behind the passenger-side tire, and waited.

In the few short seconds before the soldiers showed up, I thought of my family. For the first time, I wondered what would become of them. Would they be punished for my crimes? I felt selfish for not listening to my father, but I knew that he would understand deep down. After all, he and my mother had raised me to be the independent person I was.

The sound of the approaching vehicles pierced my ears like a freight train as they closed in. My intention was to stall them for as long as I could, but with only the pistol to retaliate, I knew my standoff would be short-lived. I accepted my fate of death.

I soon found out that death would have been much more merciful then what I was about to face. I fired

off several shots before I was shot in the shoulder. They showed me no mercy as they tied me up and beat me and then threw me in the back of a truck.

They searched my vehicle thoroughly but found no children. The general's handsome face was now filled with rage as he ordered the soldiers to head out afoot to look for the children. They had no idea about Lenz, and it was all I could do to keep from grinning. Our plan had gone terribly wrong, but in my heart, I knew the children would be safe.

This hunch was reaffirmed many times over the next several months during the general's weekly visits to my windowless cell. He tortured me viciously, and his question was always the same. "Where are they?" he would scream over and over as he beat me.

During my captivity, I was tortured, raped, urinated on, and stripped of my last bits of pride. I was exposed to the harshest elements of humanity. My incarceration only cultivated my hatred for

them, and I was constantly enticed by the desire to express it. However, out of pure stubbornness on my part, the screams of agony from the pain they inflicted were the only reply they ever got. They deserved no explanation for my actions. I had learned long before that once a man's mind is corrupted, he cannot be swayed back to the other side. Anything I said to them would only be wasted on their ignorance.

Days, weeks, and months passed as I lay in that cell, slowly dying. I was given nothing but scraps of bread to eat and a bucket of filthy water to drink from until I no longer had the desire or strength to do so. Close to the end, I realized that human life must be a great gift from God. Why else would we fight so hard to keep it?

On the morning of the day I died, the general made one last visit to my cell, and this time there was no beating. He knelt beside me and set his lantern near my head so that I could see him looking me

in the eye. The lantern flickered so brightly that opening my eyes was agonizing after being in the dark for so long; its warmth seemed foreign.

He told me that I reeked of filth and death, and he gave me one last opportunity to tell him where the children were. If I did, I would get the chance to say good-bye to my parents and beg for their forgiveness. "Wouldn't it be better for your mother and father to give you a proper burial," he said, "a chance to mourn your death? Don't you at least owe them that after the way you have humiliated them?"

I mustered my last bit of strength to answer him. I smiled and told him in a whisper that the children were safely out of his grasp. I asked him how the fight was coming along. I'd heard talk through the walls that foreign legions were making headway into Hitler's territory. Then I spit in the general's

face. He rose to his feet, kicked me in the stomach, and then walked away. My smile remained intact.

I lay in darkness again as his lantern
swayed out of sight…until, I found
my own light in the darkness.

Chapter 6

That life was now only a memory, a small part of me. Its pain would remain in a piece of my soul, but it would not define me or be the conclusion of my existence. Rather, it guided me to an understanding of life that I hadn't known before. It filled me with the sort of knowledge that can only be learned through experiences in a flawed world. It also showed me that people can break you and destroy all that you love; they can strip you of your pride and your heritage. They can take away

your freedom and even your life, but that does not mean they win.

As I watched what the afterlife had in store for those who had fallen into this evil scheme, the magnitude of the punishment they would suffer was far worse than any pain they could face on earth. I am incapable of explaining or even comprehending the sheer harshness of the existence they would endure. As much as I hated these people and what they did to their victims, including myself, I could not help but mourn their eternal fate.

All the peace of heaven that I had experienced was lost in the realization of hell and all its hopeless occupants. They had chosen a path enriched by greed and power. On earth, they had sacrificed others' lives for their personal gain. They had plagued others with suffering and felt justified in doing so. They never asked forgiveness of their creator, only praise from their mentor. Only now, in the midst of hell, would they realize his betrayal.

Satan had no equals, only prisoners—victims. Each was a prize he'd stolen from God, one more soul to torment for all eternity. He found satisfaction in their agony and in the expansion of his kingdom.

Chapter 7

My surroundings changed, and I felt a deep sense of sorrow in my soul. I stood beside my parents as they learned of my death. Hopelessness, anger, and despair consumed them. My father's strong hands quivered as they stroked my mother's hair. All the emotions they felt coursed through me as though they were my own: regret, guilt, and inadequacy. The months of agony since I was imprisoned had aged them. Their faces were more worn than I remembered, and their eyes were weary.

I wanted to embrace them, tell them I was okay, and show them the splendor that awaited them. In this moment, I felt closer to my parents and appreciated them more than ever before. In their reality, I had never been farther away. I wanted their pain to cease. And I wanted them to feel and understand the peace I experienced. If only they could see that I hadn't died in vain, but rather from doing something that they believed in just like I did.

Since my arrival here, this was the first time I felt incapable of achieving a task that I so desired. I felt utterly helpless, and then the presence of my creator came upon me. His reassuring voice told me to embrace my parents and share my peace with them.

My mother had collapsed to the floor, and my father lay by her side, cradling her. I knelt beside them and summoned from within my soul all the

peace of heaven. I was lost in the moment, but I could feel their souls touching my own.

My mother's crying subsided. She and my father gazed into each other's eyes with bewilderment, both overtaken by a peace and warmth that was unobtainable in the world they lived in. They no longer looked mournful. They felt my peace and understood it. My parents knew I had gone but that I wasn't far away.

I felt privileged to be a part of such wonder and to know that my parents had received this miracle. Their mourning would continue throughout their lives, but now the reassurance of our reunion would fill the void. The anticipation for our reunion would guide them through the remainder of their life's journey.

The love of that world had seemed trivial, unsustainable, and almost pathetic during my life on earth. I now recognized that although the love of humankind is masked and incapable of revealing

its full meaning, it was the strongest love. It was even stronger than the love of heaven because it wasn't easy to overcome the difficulty of relaying and accepting love on earth. There were often too many barriers and uncertainties surrounding people for them to receive it for all that it is.

Chapter 8

I had but one desire left before my visit to this world was over. I needed to know the outcome of the three nameless children whose lives had once been placed in my hands.

The sound of laughter rang out, and joy filled me as I looked over a comfortable farmhouse and saw a family preparing dinner with three welcome additions. The children, Alexander, Ezra, and Eliana, were no longer orphans but beloved members of a blessed family. Everything that I had hoped would happen for them was now a reality.

I felt confident that everyone I had left behind would be fine. The war would be over soon, and their journeys would continue. They would face heartache and triumph throughout their lives, but they would not do it alone. They had many of us guiding them through the lessons of life that lay before them like stepping stones of experience and knowledge. There would be a moment in time when our puzzle would be complete and our existence fulfilled.

It was time for me to embrace the continuation of my soul—to explore my past and my future. There were no constraints on the opportunities ahead. A grand adventure stood before me, and my soul yearned for the knowledge that awaited me there!

About the Author

Hillary R. Carraway has been married for ten years, and she has three children. She and her husband, Darren, raise cattle as the owners and operators of Northwest Livestock Brokers LLC. Hillary was raised in the small town of Challis, Idaho and has a great love of the outdoors and the many simple things of life. Her most savored time is that spent with her family doing chores together, working with their cattle and horses. She is motivated to teach her children the love of God while conveying to them the importance of accepting people of all religious and spiritual backgrounds.

Hillary has spent a lifetime trying to broaden her understanding of humankind and striving not to judge anyone for his or her personal beliefs. She has experienced an expansive variety of spiritual encounters that led her to create *Soul Existence.* These experiences also inform her unique views of life and death.

Printed in the United States
By Bookmasters